Woody Guthrie

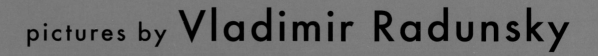

pictures by Vladimir Radunsky

WALKER BOOKS
AND SUBSIDIARIES
LONDON • BOSTON • SYDNEY

You stick out your little hand
To every woman, kid and man,

And you wave it up and down, howdi do, howdi do.
Yes, you wave it up and down, howdi do.

Howjee, heejee,
Howdi do,
Howdi doosle,
Howdi do,
Howjee, hojee,

hijee, hojee,
sir, doodle-doo.
doodle-doozie,
howdi do.
heejee, hijee,
Howdi do!

When you walk in my door
I will run across my floor,

And I'll shake you by the hand, howdi do, howdi do.
Yes, I'll shake it up and down, howdi do.

Chorus:

Howjee, heejee, hijee, hojee,
Howdi do, sir, doodle-doo.

Howdi doosle, doodle-doozie,
Howdi do, howdi do.

Howjee, hojee, heejee, hijee,
Howdi do!

On my sidewalk on my street,
Everybody that I meet,

I will shake them by the hand, howdi do, howdi do.
Yes, I'll shake it up and down, howdi do.

Chorus:

Howjee, heejee, hijee, hojee,
Howdi do, sir, doodle-doo.

Howdi doosle, doodle-doozie,
Howdi do, howdi do.

Howjee, hojee, heejee, hijee,
Howdi do!

When I first jump out of bed,
Out my window goes my head,

And I shake it up and down, howdi do, howdi do.
Yes, you shake it up and down, howdi do.

Chorus:

Howjee, heejee, hijee, hojee,
Howdi do, sir, doodle-doo.

Howdi doosle, doodle-doozie,
Howdi do, howdi do.

Howjee, hojee, heejee, hijee,
Howdi do!

I feel glad when you feel good,
You brighten up my neighbourhood,

Shakin' hands with everybody, howdi do, howdi do.
Shakin' hands with everybody, howdi do.

Chorus:

**Howjee, heejee, hijee, hojee,
Howdi do, sir, doodle-doo.**

**Howdi doosle, doodle-doozie,
Howdi do, howdi do.**

**Howjee, hojee, heejee, hijee,
Howdi do!**

When I meet a dog or cat,
I will rubby-rub his back,

Shakey, shakey, shakey paw, howdi do, howdi do.
Shakin' hands with everybody, howdi do.

Howjee, heejee, hijee, hojee,
Howdi do, sir, doodle-doo.

Howdi doosle, doodle-doozie,
Howdi do, howdi do.

Howjee, hojee, heejee, hijee,
Howdi do!

For Krishna, Shiva Das, Serena and Emma — N. G.

The Publisher wishes to acknowledge the help and
support of Nora Guthrie and Judy Bell; and Bing
Broderick of Rounder Records in the publication
of this book.

First published 2000 by Walker Books Ltd
87 Vauxhall Walk, London SE11 5HJ

10 9 8 7 6 5 4 3 2 1

Printed in Italy

The pictures in this book were done in gouache and collage.
This book has been typeset in Futura Medium.

British Library Cataloguing in Publication Data
A catalogue record for this book is available from the British Library.
ISBN 0-7445-5672-4

For more information about Woody Guthrie,
please contact the Woody Guthrie Archives at
250 West 57th Street, Suite 1218, New York, NY 10107, USA